MIDNIGHT
MEDITATIONS

The After- Hours Poetry Devotional

SHAMAIRA SMITH

A Multi Author Conglomeration

Midnight Meditations

A Multi Author Conglomeration

Midnight Meditations

Dedication

For all of us, who are but solitary travelers in this weary world.
Focus your heart on what matters the most-
Your eternal relationship with
The Father, Son, and Holy Ghost.

Peace, for us all

Sister, thank you for lending me your book
Where the sidewalk ends.

For "**I AM**"

Forward

Within these pages you will discover a rumination journey. This is the process of carefully thinking something over, pondering it, or meditating.
☆ *This is the point of Midnight Meditations* ☆

The Bible shows us many ways where Jesus distinctively used and described particular elements like earth, water, bread, and light. With an 'out-of-this-world' dialog, he turned them into unique metaphors that poetically expressed divine truth.
☆ *This is the purpose of Midnight Meditations* ☆

Welcome

Table of Contents

☆Appreciate the night, for it ushers in the opportunity to start over in the daylight☆

☆Appreciate the night, for it ushers in the opportunity to start over in the daylight ☆

☆<u>Glory-Us in Disaster</u>   67

☆<u>Another Dimension</u>   111

Continued

☆Appreciate the night, for it ushers in the opportunity to start over in the daylight ☆

☆<u>A Cry In The Night</u>   135

Introduction To the Night

Appreciate the night, for it ushers in the opportunity to start over in the daylight

*A*desperate call out in the night, in need of relief from a lifelong plight. One after another the struggling world is overwhelmed. Insomniacs from far and near search for the slightest bit of peace and mental release. Here, we are open late for the travelers of the night. For those times when your mind keeps going and your heart is restless from the fight. Pick this up when you are at your wits end, in the middle of the night when you can't go out or phone a friend. This book can be your rescue solution bringing God's peace as a midnight resolution.

Twilight hours bring about a different awareness to the senses. Being awake during this special period can often ignite genuine moments of prayer. These pages were specially prescribed for the *midnight wanderer* as a tool of faith to reach for in the restless hour of your own midnight. Biblical promises are eased into the mind to enlighten your mood and challenge your attitude.

"For the word of God is living and active, sharper than any two-edged sword, piercing to the division of soul and of spirit, of joints and of marrow, and discerning the thoughts and intentions of the heart."

(Hebrews 4:12)

Because the word of God is transformational, this book becomes divine. It is not meant to be read like your typical dated devotional. Instead, each time you pick it up, what you read is the devotion *you* need at that moment. If you listen closely, you'll surely hear a quiet whisper of peace directed at you from the Spirit of God. When you invite the Lord into your space He will refresh, refill, and usher in a reposed state of being. Each passage will intentionally direct you to keep your mind stayed on Him. In this way, wherever you find yourself mentally, extraordinary comfort can be received.

Take this time to elevate and allow your consciousness to rise into the stars and soar high above the current title waves of life. Let it move you to drift softly into the calm waters that are waiting on the *other side* of adversity. It's okay to allow your mind to *change* the subject at this hour. You are permitted to let yourself ingest this pause as you finally slow your pace and receive. Now is your appointed time to expand the unopened crevices in the back of your mind. Feel the gentle breeze of a peace that surpasses all understanding. Allow it to flow directly to you. Relax in the stillness and reach for your calm in the secret tranquility of a *holy word* spoken at the right time in the darkness.

This time was set apart for weary travelers just like you.
Take heed, for another day is soon approaching where you will need the energy that you find here to get through the next 24 hours. I want

to leave you with a gentle reminder. God knows *exactly* where you are and what you need. He is more than able to meet you in the midst of the moment. He is the antidote, the midnight medicine, the true comforter of our souls. When you allow yourself to receive from the Spirit of God, you will begin to experience that long awaited exhale. As you read, may you receive a special peace that is only found in HIM.

Matthew 11:28-30

Jesus said,

"Come to Me, all you who are weary and carry heavy burdens, and I will give you rest. Take my yoke upon you and let Me teach you, because I am humble and gentle at heart, and in me you will find rest for your souls."

Your Will

When the day fizzles out
And the quiet night goes still

I will praise you in advance
For your good and perfect will

Dreams evoke visions of twisted mind play
Which develop the tale
Of the approaching new day

Be it sleep or awake I've decided to take
One step at a time
Followed by a big leap of faith

For although many questions stir in my heart still
I must always remember that nothing happens
Outside of your good and perfect will.

Jeremiah 29:11

"For I know the plans I have for you," declares the Lord,
"Plans to prosper you and not to harm you,
plans to give you a hope and a future."

Spend The Night

In the night there's no limits to what your faith can achieve

Night is the blank slate from which your future will proceed

Night is not the time to be stuck in yesterday

Even though some things take more than twelve hours to go away

But If you spend the night in just the right way

It prepares your heart to confront the next day.

Psalm 1

… But his delight is in the Law of the LORD and on His law he meditates day and night. He is like a tree planted by streams of water, yielding its fruit in season, whose leaf does not wither, and who prospers in all that he does.

Elements

Madyanis Santiago Díaz

Water carries all our hopes
To the vast ocean of possibilities
Where Earth holds our bonds
And nourishes our certainties

Air flows through our lungs
Surrounding our body's fragility
While Fire sparkles in our blood
Like rubies that dance with fluidity

There is the intangible universe
Essence that travels in anonymity
As space and time through any verse
And in any living sparkle of humanity.

Forgiveness

In forgiveness you give up your claim to vengeance
Plans for retaliation are subsequently fenced
And giving the situation to God doesn't always make sense

Consequently, our human nature yearns for retribution
I'll get 'em back is the chanted solution

But one thing remains… the *right* thing to do
Yes. It's true this should have never happened to you
And your mind wants to erase every civilized virtue

Yet, the moral of it all is to discover a free personal gift
One that turns your spirit around and gives your soul a lift
Forgiveness does not change the facts about what has already occurred
And you don't have to surrender your *desire* to see justice served

Releasing the situation to God opens the gates to a different freedom
The road less traveled is where personal justice is won.

1 Corinthians 4:5

Therefore do not go on passing judgment before the time, but wait until
the Lord comes who will both bring to light the things hidden in the
darkness and disclose the motives of men's hearts; and then each man's
praise will come to him from God.

In Love

They would be as in love with you as I am
Bound by a deeper love, simply love

Taking the time to flex my toes in your over sized shoes
I know it's impossible to grasp your full magnitude
But all of me yearns to try

The oasis that makes up the flowology of biology
The being that put forth all existence that's studied so objectively
Surface level knowledge based on only what the eyes can see

Yet, you've thought of every tiny detail in this wondrous land
Even placed swirls of distinction at the tip of each hand

If they could only grasp a moment of your magnitude
Or understand the smallest component of your attitude

Or even touch the intelligence within your invincible hand
Then *they* would be as in love with you as I am
Bound by a deeper love, simply Love.

Calignment

☆Come into alignment with the calling assignment of Matthew 28:19☆

Despondent and dignified, yet dogmatized is this incontrovertible
Truth, while strangers whisper absurdity
As they deplore this public preaching roost
Overcome by destiny I stand and apply a reverberant code
CALIGNMENT is for all to see reflecting the Bible so bold

I embellish and assimilate the ancient morsels that I've heard
I mitigate the Biblical mystery of this perennial immutable word
Expeditiously I turn the pages in unison as I psychosomatically mix
Prayer into this interwoven communication which
Emphatically flips your switch

For within the confines of these definitive pages the Bible expounds
upon light, and for me this is contagious in many stages as
I live out your word in hindsight

I'm silently filling up on Spirit adoring You on this night
For at the dawn when daylight speaks, I metaphorically intend to
Pound the streets holding a Heaven sent passage, so easy to understand
Behold an unrelenting messenger with a message
To spread across the land.

Dreams

Sleeping is always a mystery
A required shut down for the body

When your brain is most active during REM sleep
This is the time to enter in
This involuntary mind journey
Of images sensation and pure emotion

Sometimes a dream is more than it seems
Reality is captured in a vision
Thus to wake up and remember it
Can cause a double world collision

But just how far will your dreams let you go?
Wake up and try to live them out
And only then can you know.

Image attribution: A guide to dreams by Monica Chinsami (puffy.com)

The 5 Types Of Dreams

Normal Dreams

Common dreams about people and experiences that we can sometimes forget.

Day Dreams

When we escape from reality and visualize the past, present, and future throughout the day.

Lucid Dreams

Being completely aware and in control of the dream you are having while you sleep.

False Awakening Dreams

A vivid type of dream that feels like you have woken up but you're actually still asleep.

Nightmares

The least favorite type of dream. Nightmares are disturbing and scary dreams that can feel realistic.

God Night

In the twilight hours of 3am, I'm awake to the world but alone in my head, sitting still on top of my bed, a series of questions consume me W*hy* am I *awake*? Is this moment right here being recorded for Heaven's sake?

I slow down my thinking to search for an answer within my soul
Instead panic, for in just a few hours it will be time to get up and go
But breathe- for *right now* is here, it's the *present* that I'm in
I'm awake and worried about yesterday's sins
Stressing tomorrow with all the trouble that it holds within

The darkness that dwells in the late night hour
Woos me to question my own integrity and valor
I keep hearing voices telling me I'm not good enough
I *think* I do well each day on this Earth but
How do I match my deeds to a Heavenly worth?

I sigh as I quiet my thoughts and lift my confounded face to the sky
I speak in my head, *Ok God, Hi*

I don't know what else to do so I'm giving you a try
I have numerous expectations for this coming new day

Will I finish my list? Will I remember to pray? Or will my time be over at some point today? Will you appear and lift your people away? How can I make a difference with the things I say?

How am I ever going to find my way?

While this yearning for answers runs freely through my mind
I feel a reassurance that all things will happen in their due time
Perplexed, I sit there wide awake while the clock keeps ticking away
Let's face it, ready or not here comes the future A.K.A today
Laying very still in hopes of more rest, my thumping heart beats
To the rhythm of my stress
I fold my hands across my chest in the still of the new morning's air
And suddenly to my surprise a faint whisper meets me there

*Don't worry, I will always care. When you go through your day, I'll remind you to pray and give you help with the things that come your way. Don't worry about what tomorrow may bring, keep your eyes centered on me through everything. I hold you and the future too, you're so unique that I only made just one you. Stress will never get you through everything you were designed to do
Cast your cares on me, for it's my plan to work things out indefinitely.*

Some People

Some people are simply stars in this world
You know it when you meet 'em

And when they fizzle out one day
You'll realize just how much you needed them

Don't drift thru life with a frown
And rude animosity unconfined

For special people can cross your path
Time and image undefined

Be careful of your approach
Whether it is night or day

For we never know precisely when
An entertaining Angel has come our way.

Hebrews 13:1-2

Continue in brotherly love. Do not neglect to show hospitality to strangers, for by doing so some people have entertained angels without knowing it.

From Dust

There's power in being made from dust

But on sleepless nights this verse used to

Make me feel totally useless

Like distant from Heaven

Yet connected to the Earth

A lower rank to the ground we sank

A dusty reminder of our wretched worth

But these dirty eyes were opened one day

And I truly got the chance to see

That rising from the dust was actually

An anointing from the most exquisite royalty

As a tree is planted, from the ground it surely grows

We, like the seed of the tree, are *connected*

A vessel of Earth where the breath of God's glory shows.

Psalm 100:3
Know ye that the LORD *is* God. He hath made us and not we ourselves.

Quarter Till

Something comes around this hour
You'll miss it if you don't pay attention
It spirals down from outer space
It's origin quite possibly is Heaven

Seven lamp stands, seven eyes
Roam from sea to shining sea
Here to watch and observe
The nighttime actions of you and me

It comes around this hour
2AM quarter till 3
If you feel a slight chill, it's watching you still
So, what do you want them to see?

Are you up going about your business
Carrying on as if you can just dismiss this?
Or maybe you're asleep in a dream state so deep
As it passes you by without a peep
And if you happen to be up praying
There's a really good chance it will respond
To what you are saying

This isn't the last and surely not the first

That this presence drops in to visit us on Earth

So, if you weren't aware, then now you know
The eyes of the Lord travel to and fro.

2 Chronicles 16:9
For the eyes of the Lord range throughout the Earth to strengthen
those whose hearts are fully committed to him...

Supine Nostalgia

Supine nostalgia a bottle of ink spilled across the day

Not awake, not flat lined, but in a semi-conscious way

Loud silence in a world full of loud noise

Shadows linger longer in epic, eerie poise

Supine… Dreaming but not quite asleep

Nostalgia… Where deep calls unto deep

A heavenly height that was finally breached

In supine nostalgia at the climax of sleep.

Job 33:15

In a dream, a vision of the night, when sound sleep falls upon men,

while they slumber in their beds...

Blades of Grass

It stays in place as we quickly travel by
If you look closely you'll see that it reaches up for the sky

Now it could grow sideways or just plain flat on the ground
Instead it reaches for the Heavens
until someone comes and cuts it down

You could learn a lot if you stare at a firm blade of grass
But that's only if you're willing to mentally attend its class

You'd learn to stand steady and reach as life goes by fast
If you're cut down, come right back around
and aim to complete your task

No matter how long it takes or what bends or breaks, you *stand your
ground,* though the winds may change and your world may shake
And even through your greatest earthquake

Just like a field of grass you're not growing through this life alone
Stay firmly planted for God placed you here and knows where you've landed

From above comes your energy in the form of a sun (Son)
And down comes the rain to bring living water when you have none

So, keep your roots nestled deep in solid ground
Continue reaching for the sky since your help is Heaven bound

Keep pushing up through the dirt of life no matter what comes your way, even when you're stepped on and neglected
Or mowed over and thrown away

Just remember to look up like all blades of grass
And adopt what they know from their silent teaching class

That you are specially created (and built tough too)
And with God on your side you're bound to make it through.

My First Thought

ME: I tried my best, but it wasn't received, and nobody liked what I had to say

LORD: Was your heart set on pleasing them or following *me* and *my* way?

ME: I walked by faith... believed I had received... and yet, it never came to pass

LORD: Were you looking to see *my* will or your own? Because those two things can clash.

ME: I searched for treasures and came up with trash

LORD: I passed you my lens to look through, but you looked *beyond* what I gave to you.

ME: This pain I'm in has taken control, and the mountain has not moved for me

LORD: Moving a mountain one stone at a time, makes the task a little more easy.

ME: I don't have an abundant life, instead it's always heartache and strife

LORD: My grace could be sufficient for you, when you stop complaining, would you like to try a dose of that too?

ME: It never goes the way I've planned

LORD: First check with the one who has the blueprints in *HIS* hand

ME: The more things change the more stays the same. Failure should be my middle name!

LORD: There's always something to have and something to lose. Always watching for rain can give you the blues. If constant negativity is all that you see, then you can never receive your blessings from me.

Just in case you still don't get it yet, the moral here is perspective-

Change Your Mindset

James 1:17

Every good and perfect gift is from above, coming down from the Father of the heavenly lights, who does not change like shifting shadows.

Caught In an Angel's Gaze

1 Peter 1:12, Peter reveals that Angels gaze down at God's plan of redemption

The angels watch us looking down on all mankind

The angels watch us watching all of God's divine

Is it for all of God's salvation you search?

Are you just fascinated by what He did on earth?

Is it because you're trying to find our worth?

What is it you're searching for on this green Earth?

The angels watch us looking down on all mankind

The angels watch us, what are you looking down to find?

Tell me what's so intriguing about me?

Is it that you're seeking who loves God and his mercy?

What's so intriguing about me that you're peering down to see?

The angels watch us looking down on what God made

The angels watch us just like people watch a parade

Is there nowhere that we can hide from your sight?

Do you come down to our bedrooms as we sleep at night?

Are you around when people need you the most?

Do you guide us as a spirit or aid the Holy Ghost?

Why are you trying to figure me out?

Are you trying to see if I know what this life is all about?

Were you recording me inside the womb?

Just to go back and report it in the throne room?

Maybe you're searching deep inside my soul

Just to see if I will keep all of my self control

Maybe you are trying to encourage me

Just to see if I will live my life faithfully

What's so intriguing about me?

That you're peering down to see!

Luke 15:10

Likewise, I say to you, there is joy in the presence of the angels of God
over one sinner that repents

God is Good

Because God is good there is hope for tomorrow
Because God is good He provides joy in exchange for our sorrows

Because God is good all trouble must have an end
Because God is good my wounds and hurts all have a chance to mend

Because God is good I'm assured that all evil will be conquered
Because God is good I can receive strength while pressing onward

Because God is good, Heaven and Hell *both* exist
If God was not good, then there would be no reason for any of this

Because God is good there must be a brighter day
Because God is good I'm encouraged to wipe the tears away

Because our God is good- this what we *need* to say
To keep our heart and mind renewed and
In sync with his presence each day.

God is Good

All the time. And all of the time

God is Good

Palms To Heaven

In perfect contrast to the back of every hand
Lays a color that resembles the fine grains of sand
If we all just took a moment to turn our palms to the sky
Unity could block out division as different arms were raised high
When a palm turns upward in symbolic surrender
It's usually at a time when our emotions are rendered
An up facing palm speaks a nonverbal melody
A cry out, a plea, a humble action for all to see

Since a palm branch represents goodness, triumph, and victory
Then what does that say about the fleshly hand of you and me?
Measuring from the wrist to the ends of the fingers in length
Lifting open palms is not a weakness, it's a strength

Consider the open palms of Jesus as He bore them on the cross
The Bibles says the scars remain, just to reflect his ardor for us
Thus, open palms reflect many things
Yielding stories, wounds, and whatever weight that this life brings

So, if you take this moment to show God your open palm
Then it can exemplify all of humanity in one united song
Together as one people we could cause intolerance to leaven
This is what can happen when we turn our palms to Heaven.

Revealed

When Mother Nature dresses in her noir nightgown
Evening backs away so darkness can be found

If you tear the sky apart you'll see
The night is just a temporary illusion
A black out period to start over fresh
From yesterday's mistakes and confusion

But beyond this cloak of darkness
What is really staring back at you?
Instead of a 'what'
Let's consider it being a 'who'

For it is said the eyes of God
Never go to bed, instead
They search the world to see
The lifestyle decisions of you and me

I'll tell you this just once my friend
So make sure you hear me right
The evil you do in darkness
Will never be hidden from HIS sight.

1 Peter 3:12

The eyes of the Lord watch over those who do right, and his ears are open to their prayers. But the Lord turns his face against those who do evil.

Find The Lord

Stars are a puzzle in the night sky
Hanging there for all to see

It's up to you to open your mind
Exploring every possibility

The Lord is ever present
Clear as night and day

Rendering the word of truth
And lighting your path to the way

If you turn the puzzle outside in
The mystery suddenly becomes plain

You'll discover your piece is found in Him
As the Heavens reveal his name.

Psalm 19:1

The heavens declare the glory of God;

The skies proclaim the work of His hands.

Time 2 Look 4 It

Sweet revelations and eternal contemplations
For what is this life for a sinner like me?
I really disagree like in Galatians 5:17
Then John 3:16 brings me back on the scene
And my heart finds peace in one way of being

But I am yet born into the riches of this world
When Romans 12:2 tells me not to come unfurled
But to live is to want whether you like it or not
Until the time is over, this world is what we've got
We must learn to lean on Christ like Isaiah 40:31
This is a must because everyday I grow a bit more numb
Knowing that my choices will determine if and where I'll go
John 14:6 already provides a blatant, "I told you so"

Earthly rewards or frustrations for what does it all matter?
Since ultimately inhabitants on earth will face a common destiny or
disaster, as it's clearly described in Revelation fifteen's chapter
The moral of this rhyme is to cause you to *make* the time
To seek out all you can about the Bible's prophetic line
Since the gift of *now* is so exclusive and divine, we must find peace in
The moment as we spiral towards the end of time.

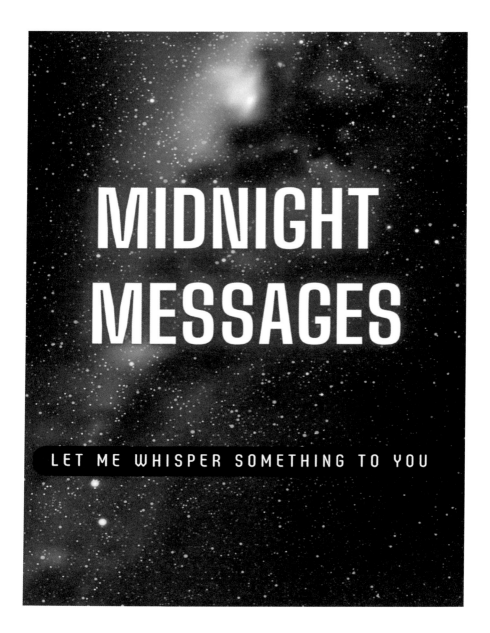

Question Mark In The Sky

If you have ever took to the sky and started in asking
Who, what, when, where, or why

Then you are the reason it is sitting there
High above, suspended in mid air

The mark of the centuries illuminates at night
Reflecting back curiosity, humanities birthright

Like a poster board or fame on display
The question mark in the sky
Poses for us the very same way.

Psalm 77:6

I will remember my song in the night; I will meditate with my heart,

and my spirit ponders...

The Tree

The seed was directed to just the right place
As the hands of angels tilled the ground and cleared the perfect space
A seedling was set into the Earth beginning the life cycle of a tree
Every day it was cared for and nurtured so delicately

The warmth of the sun hits in just the right spot
Like a warm bath towel after the shower has stopped
The breath of God blows over the top of the soil
Ensuring the perfect environment
For the sapling to sprout from its coil
It stretches its arms and grows into a young tree
And over the years its maturity spans out beautifully
It's been nurtured and pruned till just the right age
To make its debut on eternity's stage
For on one fine day when that tree was cut down
Its death made it the most useful of all the trees around

Purposed and fastened into a cross just right
At the death of the tree was the beginning of its most meaningful life
As the most meaningful life was hung on that very same tree
A death that was the most meaningful encased them both eternally
A meaningful life and a meaningful death

The magnitude of Jesus, the world will never forget.

Could you have done it?

Knowing from the beginning of time

You're nurturing the very same tree

Where a horrific death will one day be

In season you watched it get chopped down

To hoist you up high, impaled off the ground-

Could you have done it?

John 3:16

For God so loved the world, that He gave his only begotten Son, th
whosoever believeth in Him should not perish, but have everlasting li

To Rest

What does the definition of REST look like?

To rest is to set your mind at ease regardless of the circumstances
To *rest* is to take every thought captive and surrender it to the Lord's
Care

To rest is to close out the world and open up the door
To the secret place found under the shelter of the most high
To *rest* is to relinquish your backpack of worries to the prince of peace
To *rest* is the feeling of floating while angels harmonize a melody that
Calms

To *rest* is a symphony where your thoughts intertwine with spirit
To *rest* is to achieve the fullness of letting go and trusting God in all
Things.

Psalm 3:5

sleep; I wake again, because the LORD sustains me.

FaithFight

In cloak yourself in His word as you travel through the darkness of your night. Surround yourself in His presence, so that you may not be found wanting. Be confident in your God in pain, and even at the door of death. For it is He who has already prepared your table.

Stand confident in the Lord thy God, for in times when you don't understand, that can mean a miracle is working out and ready to be released from his hand. At this hour, try a new thing of just letting go.

Let go as if you're skydiving out of a plane.

Free yourself to trust Him, just like you would your parachute.

Reject all feelings that claim you will fall.

Picture yourself soaring on eagles wings high above it all.

And when you have landed safely and finally touched down, you can practice *living* by faith, since that's exactly what you used to get back on the ground. Of course life can be hard especially when we give up and settle for a pit. But with faith, you're making the choice to *choose* to come out on top of it.

Learning to trust in God is how your faith takes flight.

At this moment, feel the release, it's totally alright

Yes, now is the time to *walk by faith and not by sight*

This declaration is what we call the triumphant Faith Fight.

The Argument

I had to tell 'em one day you see, while they pointed down at my F.A.G Jesus Tee. Hovering, they formed a circle of mockery. "I like it. I like it a lot," I proclaimed. "Since I'm a fan of Jesus Christ, the most high name."

Batting an eye they frowned at me, "I admire his story but-seriously? What fool gives up his life so willingly? I could never give him any glory. Much less wear a shirt about His story!"

In their roar of laughter directed at me, I was taken back by the punch of their cruelty. Then I thought to myself, *If they don't love God, then what's it matter to me? Jesus is more impressive than the human people I ever see- Nevertheless, it'll be hell fire for you, while the saints live free!* But then something peculiar occurred to me. Their joking around was just revealing, the shallow lives of simple boasters who yearned for deeper meaning and feeling.

So, channeling courage as a voice of truth on the scene, I began to proclaim, "I don't know your beliefs but let me try to explain what I mean." I hunched my shoulders, which seemed kinda odd, but it helped when I reminded them, "There's no level we can ever rise to where we don't need God. This life is not meant to last forever, so do you need to be reborn? Come on now, we can seek him together."

Confused, they gave a quick reply, "Um, I just don't think that's right... plus I have plans to get home early tonight!"

Amused, I was like, "Awe, come on, just try! Jesus came to offer eternal life. I don't think he's impressed by what you think is right. Let me show you how to eternally win... Bow your head and confess your sin.*"*

They looked ashamed, so I quickly exclaimed, "Not to *me*! But silently from within. God will hear you directly when you call out to Him."

They stayed, and we prayed after a few awkward moments went by, "Jesus hear our prayers," (I looked up to the sky). "We silently cry out to you, please save these folks and guide them too. Help them receive clear direction from you and reveal your salvation to help them start over brand new."

Dropping their hands in silent relief, they put a skip in their step and scurried down the street. I took in the moment and putting on a smile, I found myself standing there for a while.

Living for Christ you'll face opposition, and with all these lost souls, nothing's gained if you just dismiss them. Sometimes an argument creates the perfect space to meet. (I realized this through the *thump-dump* of my heart beat). Similar to a sidewalk designed to take you someplace, God ordains each person's path so he can meet them face to face.

Psalms 1:1-3

Blessed is the man who walks not in the counsel of the wicked, nor stands in the way of sinners, nor sits in the seat of scoffers; but his delight is in the law of the Lord, and on his law he meditates day and night. He is like a tree planted by streams of water that yields its fruit in season...

Birth Day & Night

The spirit of life has found you again
And counted you alive among the living
Just like that another year is what you're getting

This relevant 365 day cycle catches
Every individual in their own 24 hours
This time is special to call your own
The designated day in which you were born

The day of your birth could have happened at night
Doubling your release into a world of little light
But no matter the hour your presence makes it clear
You light up the world because you were meant to be here
Prime in the cycle of yet another year

So if this happens to be the night of your birth
Relax and reflect what your life means on Earth
And a solemn shout goes out to you
Happy Birthday Blessings!
And may you accomplish everything
You were sent here to do.

Psalm 139:14
I praise you because I am fearfully and wonderfully made...

Un~Noticed

Not one sparrow falls to the ground

Unnoticed

Not one hair falls from your head

Unnoticed

Every deed you do for God will never go

Unnoticed

He is a God of justice so no evil goes

Unnoticed

The tears you cry in the dark do not go

Unnoticed

The requests on your heart will never be

Unnoticed

This tiny word between bold lines does not go

Unnoticed

Even Satin's rants and requests did not go

Unnoticed

Our praise and worship is inhabited and does not go

Unnoticed

The grass grows and seasons change which never go

Unnoticed

This life is already arranged, so that precious YOU could never be

Unnoticed

Liquid Steps

Standing here alone looking out over a vast ocean. All navigational coordinates would reveal only one human in this exact location. Yet, there's a multitude of people in this world, vast as the waters of the sea. A whole ocean of variety and opportunity. This life reflects a current of ever changing waves that challenge our very existence. The endless expanse resembles this life and the many directions it can lead.

A sea of possibilities to venture into, where the waves are always inviting you in and calling you closer to the deep end. I want to stick my feet in but the further I go, the deeper it gets. Too cautious to take a chance and see what will come out of my actions.
What if I go too far? I may drown in my failure.
What if I don't try? I may regret it forever.

The heart is always longing for more yet only uncertainties are certain. In the ever changing movement on the surface of the water, an image of the calm sky is reflecting from above. The endless sky that covers it all, is perfectly set up to bring my mind right back to you. You who are above it all, giving us the blessed assurance that no matter how far we may travel, or whether life is deep or shallow- you are always there above it all to cover every liquid step or fall.

Psalm 23:1-3

The Lord is my shepherd; I shall not be in want. He makes me lie down in green pastures, He leads me beside quiet waters, He restores my soul.

One Peculiar Rock

*O*ut of all the millions and billions of people in the world, *you* stand out exclusively among the numbers. Hello You. The one reading this sentence *right now.* Yes! I'm talking directly to you only. Sometimes it may be a struggle to believe that God even notices *you* or can actually hear your prayers amidst all of the noise. To dive deeper into my point, let's conduct a small comparison using rocks for example. Like people, rocks fill the Earth in uncountable numbers and yet, neither one has an identical match. The same way it takes time for humans to grow, there is a process for rocks as well. Another similarity can be found in the variety of shapes and sizes.

Rocks, (just like people) can be found everywhere you turn. Some rocks are picked for concrete to become a solid foundation for the bigger picture. Others are made into jewelry and decorated as precious stones. Then you have some that sit in their place in a patient state of waiting to be chosen. One basic similarity with rocks and people is that each one is actually purposed for a reason. I can recall this one particular stone that laid in wait for years, never knowing he would be picked to smash into the forehead of Goliath. Yet at the right time, it was chosen. It played a major role in a powerful story that has been remembered for generations.

Although this stone felt lost and forgotten among many, it was always well known by God. Its direct location and season had already been predestined. In the waiting, it was exactly where it needed to be for God to use it for great things. On that one particular day, this one peculiar stone lived out its one particular purpose.

The same goes for *you*. Be patient in the waiting and don't stray from the good course. God sees *you* right where *you* are. Your life is not a mistake and he has not forgotten about *you*. There is a reason that *you* were made distinctively peculiar. It's because he created *you* with a particular purpose that only *you* can fulfill.

☆ Let this stand as your personal reminder of that ☆

Luke 12:27

...Are not five sparrows sold for two pennies?
Yet not one of them is forgotten by God. And even the very hairs of
your head are all numbered, so do not be afraid;
you are worth more than many sparrows.

AGAPE

Already knowing that the love will not be returned

Unconditional love

Knows all your moves and sees the sin that soils the soul

Unyielding love

Premeditated grace given to you even though you do not deserve to receive it

Unshakable love

Remains no matter how many times you turn away, open arms are here to stay

Unwavering love

Already decides to give a second chance even before you decide to ask

Unrelenting love

Laid down his life for you, knowing you'd refuse to live your life for him

Undying love

Cares to keep a watchful eye upon you, even though you care only for yourself

Unbreakable love

Loves you whether you want it or not, he's just not ever going to stop

Unstoppable love

I Called It Sunshine

I called it sunshine, but you called it a plan of mine
It felt like sunshine, but
You called it love

I woke up early and called it a new morning
I watched an eagle fly and heard my children snoring
As I read the paper I called it mother nature
And as I sipped my coffee I heard you call it love

I called it sunshine, but you called it a plan of mine
At first it felt like sunshine, but you
Made me feel loved.

Psalm 27: 14

God my savior, my hope is in you all the day long.

Lightning Faith

It started off as a tiny chocolate-gray cloud rolling in from the south that evening. I made it home just in time to take cover from the dark mocha sky. A brewing dust storm began to sweep across the desert like an eerie tornado. I tucked myself inside and prepared for an unsettling night ahead. After an hour of violently swirling winds, I peeked out the window to see if the dust had finally settled. When I opened the back door, a cool desert breeze met my face. The smell of freshly fallen rain on a dry and thirsty land was strangely invigorating to the senses. It called me to step out and linger a while in the pleasant after breeze. I must say, nature's invitation was hard to resist, although the hint of danger was still lingering in the atmosphere. I glanced over my shoulder to the right and just above the neighbor's house, I caught a glimpse of exotic lightning that appeared to be rolling closer by the second. Aware of the danger, I just couldn't resist the urge to linger a bit longer underneath the cover of my backyard patio. Taking a deep breath of the thirst-quenched air, I watched the clouds light up as the vibrant lightning show pummeled towards me. Desert storms are always amazing, but this time something was different. The atmosphere around me was serene and majestic, just like a movie scene right before the magic begins to happen.

Suddenly, across the back yard it began raining in one particular spot. As this mystical shower flowed from Heaven, all I could do was marvel at the God of wonders as I watched nature unfold all around me. I wanted to sing praises in the moment, but instead I chose to stand in awe and silently adore him. I shed a tear behind the mystery of such a marvelous being. In that moment it became obvious that my admiration was noticed on high. The lightning grew more intense as it circled around my home. Every flash was so fierce, that it lit up the dark night as if it were high noon. So much so, that I was able to get a clear visual of my surroundings. Each flash lasted for an abnormally long period, but I stood firm and did not retreat. I began to think about how dangerous it was for me to be standing here so vulnerable at this moment. Then it dawned on me, I was actually too afraid to move. My fear was not just in reference to this storm, but afraid of stepping into *all* of life's storms in general. I thought about what Peter must have felt in the storm on the boat that night. His heart was obviously willing to step out, but he needed Jesus to give him a verbal confirmation in order to actually *move* forward. When he gathered up the courage to call out, 'Lord, can I come to you?' I believe Peter knew that Jesus realized exactly what his request meant; if I step out, do you *really* got me? Will you really *protect* me? Will you actually *catch* me if I start to sink?

Jesus provided all that Peter needed by telling him to come. In awe, I mentally reminded God about this, and how I now (like Peter then) needed confirmation to step off of this porch (and not just my patio porch but every other ledge I was standing at in life). If I stepped out into the storm, would he come to *my* aid as well? I cried this out to the chocolate-gray sky as the rain continued to fall in one place. The lightning grew more fierce as it threatened to land on my head from above. The scary part was not knowing what to expect, and if the worst *did* happen, what would I do about it? Would anyone find me if I was struck by lightning out here? As I teetered on the edge of the concrete step, sixty percent of me wanted to step off of that porch and out into the night storm. The other forty percent fought against my will, giving me every reason not to budge, rendering me temporarily paralyzed. Then I remembered the magnitude of who I was actually talking to out there. The same God who has kept me in the worst of times and promised to be with me always. As this realization entered into my spirit, I felt the Lord tell me, "How will you ever see my protection if you never step out? How can you even measure or know for sure if I will be there for you if you are too afraid to come into the storm where I am already at?"

As if my own spirit had pushed me from behind, I stepped off the ledge and went out. Forty-nine percent afraid, but fifty-one percent willing to try God and see him (seeing me) out in the rain. With lightning dramatically flashing, I stomped away from the safety of my porch. Barefooted, I marched the entire seven yards to my back fence and touched it proudly. When I courageously turned around to make my way back to the porch, a vicious flash of lightning was right there waiting for me. I started to close my eyes but then my spirit said, "No! When your eyes are closed, you only see darkness. Keep them open so that you are fully looking to God's light."

Impressed, I tossed fear to the corner (who was still walking with me, but I ignored it because my hope was on something stronger to shield me) and pressed onward. When I reached the porch my knees buckled as I looked back on what I had accomplished. In what I thought was the most dangerous of situations, I realized I had made it because He *wanted* me to. On my knees I asked, "So, is this what you want us to do in these last days? Step boldly into the storm and see *you* instead of the threatening dangers all around?"

This time my reply came in the comfort of a gentle wind. Receiving my affirmation, I looked up at the cumulus cloud-filled night as the sparkling stars poked through the gaps in the clouds to peer down at the Earth. I finally began to understand how God wants us to respond to the lightning in the storm-

It's an unshakable faith, in Him.

Psalm 51:10

Create in me a clean heart, O God, and renew a steadfast spirit in me

GLORY~US

IN

DISASTER

IN THE MIDST OF TROUBLED TIMES
WE ALL NEED PEACE

Zephaniah 3:17

The LORD your God is in your midst, a mighty one who will save; He will rejoice over you with gladness; He will quiet you by his love; He will exult over you with loud singing.

Darkness Is His Light

Tamara G. Smith

When most people think of darkness they think of the night
But I think of pain and struggle that God will make alright
It's one thing to have faith, the substance to believe and not see
But it's a completely different thing when He shows himself to me
Through a smile from a stranger on one of my toughest days
Or the glimmer of glitter from a sunset's sun rays

Through a helping hand when I'm down on my luck
Or making a way out of no way when I feel hopeless and stuck
Through the darkness He shines his light
But you have to believe
That the Great I Am is all you will ever need

I've been beaten and bruised by this world
To the point where living felt like dying
But with the last of my strength I run to Him crying
Where His love for me is *real* and the comfort is undenying

Where He loves me enough that He blessed me to see
All of the many times He's revealed himself to me
The dark isn't intimidating you see
Because He uses the dark for my testimony.

Glorious Disaster

Oh what a glorious disaster to come!

The air whispers and the mornings hum
Daydreams remind me while I try to brace for impact
The future is now so get ready to fight back

With every sun rise or even sunset
Only the Father of time knows what event comes next
Echoes of hate welcome us to The End of Days
And if you are reading this now you're probably not amazed

Same way we detect the coming of a new season
The hint of *change* is in the air and we all know the reason
The world is wicked just as second Timothy describes
All things must be fulfilled so look out for the signs

Patient endurance will be required for saints like you and me
This glorious disaster will come about all so suddenly
There's persecution ahead for righteousness' sake
The sky will crack and the earth will *shake*
But none of these things will cause me to dread

For the Lord will return for his people
Just like He said.

Blessed Assurance

Matthew 28:20

And behold, I am with you always, even to
the end of the age…

Dark Lights

Purple, light Gray, trickle-trickle, shiny, clear
If night colors made a sound then this is what you'd hear

Pale White, Red, Indigo, the deepest shade of Blue
Blended together make darkness, so black you won't see through

Peach, Yellow, Orange, and Neon all hold and reflect their position
While crystal flashes of light prove the darkness
can't out switch 'em

For the God of light saw fit to make the dark
But since He's a consuming fire the darkness loses all heart.

Genesis 1:5

God called the light day, and the darkness He called night. And there was evening and there was morning, One day.

Gone In The Morning

He clothes the lilies of the field, but in due season

their garments will be gone in the morning

This too shall pass, it won't be long before you see the final wave

crash, and the perishable perish then wear out in a flash

The day will come for you to sing a new song

And all that's right will emerge from all that went wrong

It can't rain forever all things must surrender

If it's gone now don't dwell on the how

Simply yield life its well deserved bow

All things have a time limit or destined plateau

Since change never changes

What's here now will one day also go

This is life's heartbeat the equator of common ground

No matter your status what's one day up

Will eventually come falling down.

He clothes the lilies of the field, but in due season

their garments will be gone in the morning

Luke 12:26-28

... Consider how the lilies grow; They do not labor or spin. Yet I tell you, not even Solomon in all his glory was adorned like one of these. If that is how God clothes the grass of the field, which is here today and tomorrow is thrown into the furnace, how much *more* will He clothe you, O you of little faith!

Search & Recovery

Create in me a clean heart, O God, & renew a steadfast spirit within me , Psalm 51:10

Can your heart search for God in the dark night season?
Putting smiles aside and brighter days away
Let's completely avoid the stigma of *have a nice da*y
I'm referring to times when you're attitude's thick with malice
When you woke up on one, and you speak to no one
And you hear your spirit proclaim, "*Im done*"

Yeah, in that dark box where we argue with defeat
And resemble the complete opposite of meek
When we throw up our hands refusing God's plans
And anger takes over with unlimited commands
Yes, you are getting closer to the deep end
Of the dark place, but since everyone's different
I'll let you fill in your *own* steps to disgrace

Existing in the shadow of darkness you start to believe the lie
That in your particular situation God has turned a blind eye
Thus, back to the question that was posed for a reason
Can your heart search for God in the dark night season?
If not then you must learn to try
Only then will you discover the value in your own reason why.

Muted Cries Heard

Jennifer Adams (angel23gp@hotmail.com)

Feeling delusional, lost in my mind in a wave of emotional thoughts
Lost of words to express my feelings; sadness grips my heart without
tears. In the middle of the night sitting at my table listening to
"Just a prayer away"

And wondering *why* as dyssomnia fully sets in. Wondering if He hears
my muted cries. Speechless from the low blows of life; wondering if I
should get up or even *how.* Where do I start? Is it really worth it?
Life with invisible pain. Burdened with depression, grief, guilt, &
sorrow. So low to the ground I thought death was on the horizon

But it's just another morning; *HELP* was the only word muffled all
night. The morning arrived but it's a brand new day and years have
passed. Obstacles have been overcome, valleys lead to hill peaks,
Deserts turned to rivers

Now, sitting at a different table at night right before bed in reflection
of my life and where I've been; Tears begin to flow heavy from my
eyes as I realize He heard me.

Inspired By ☆ Psalm 34

Darkness Falls

When darkness falls the mind
Harbors many evils of the day
Spiritual sword stab through flesh of clay

Moon blinks twice leaving half an eyelid open
The heartbeat of the night
With violence and wonder unspoken

Millions of tiny molecules of
Only the highest resolution
Can create a dense color called
Night, the dark illusion

Puzzle of destiny future and past
Each star yields a story
Hidden in the dark sea of broken glass.

Psalm 112:4
Even in darkness light dawns for upright, gracious, compassionate,
righteous men

Is There A Hero?

Some days are just plain bad consumed
Overall with the thickness of sad
As evening closes in, I'm forced to forget the day
Instead I'll speak to you 'O night, and this is what I have to say

On my side of the world there are no bright spaces

War and poverty looms over grief stricken faces
The atmosphere matches our shattered broken hearts
Who will answer our cries and bring us new starts?
While the preachers keep on speaking, all cheery and upbeat
The rest of us suffer at the hands of defeat
Where is the King of the world whose mercies have no end?
Over here you seem absent like a long distance friend

Is this life nothing more than an entertaining game?
Where the people are near accents to an unknown aim?
Some people seem to have a winning contract
While others are helpless or just simply held back
And this struggle goes beyond the things that they lack

So as I speak to this night with my cries of gloom
I send my request on Angel's wings directly to the throne room
I will wait and see if you rescue the people who look like me
And when you show up, only then, I will have my testimony.

Flicker Of Flame

Spirit of bright on dark surface

Watching fire dance at night

Lures the senses to deeper purpose

Used in Heaven to burn of glory and fame

The internal blaze of Jesus' eyes

Is likened to a fiery flame

Hell's inferno the second death, so hot and vicious

Lake of fire consumes the captives

Burning up all hopes and wishes

Look at it deeper, can you hear the screams?

Yet in the blue blaze of orange a bit of Heaven so serene

Fire cannot be manufactured only just ignited

It helps, it hurts, it's hated, and invited

Element eternal existing in three realms

It's very presence transforms, overtakes, and overwhelms

It tries you, refines you, and reveals the work inside you

A flicker of flame lights the darkest dimension

The creator of this is obviously full of viciously wonderful inventions

Something so magnificently special about this light

The mind can't help but wonder when you watch it dance at night.

Hebrews 12:29

For our God is a consuming fire

Not Done

Despair- a haunting presence that won't let me go
Heart ache- a pain that I only wish I didn't know

Confusion- wondering what it's all even worth
Giving up- just ready to go away from this Earth

With this I sense myself drawing close to an end
I take the hand of depression, my dark secret friend

Since life and loss is never perfectly clear
I get to make the choice on where I go from here

With nothing left to lose all I control is my decision
Up or down, either way will just cause more division

Reality stings like a dagger to the heart
But I remember someone said calamity can light the spark

So maybe this trouble exists only to ignite a flame
That prompts the weary to call upon Jesus' name.

Matthew 11:28-29

Come to me, all who are weary, faint, and carry heavy burdens, and I will give you REST. Take my yoke upon you and learn from me, because I am humble and gentle, and in ME, you will find rest for your souls.

He Looks Upon Me

Even in my weakest hour He looks upon me
There are times where I feel alone
Times when I wonder if He's given up after all that I've done wrong
Times when my flesh gets so weak, my hands get dirty
And my mouth needs to be cleaned from the words I speak

Times when I find myself in shame
Times when it's everyone else I choose to blame
In my ego I get all wrapped up in the wrong plan
Then I find myself trapped like a snake in quicksand
My circumstances make me pause and think
Could God still care while I'm covered in all this stink?

Guilt makes me see how far I have sunk
How I tossed away hope and on sin got drunk
I don't want to deal with myself this way
I don't even think I can go on another day
So, I'll distance myself and hide away
Yet, through it all we have to remember
In times of floods and times of failure

That God is still willing to hold our hand on the way down
So that when we are ready to get u
We are *already* found

Through the ashes and with the muck
The Holy Spirit whispers gently,
Come on and get up

In our weakest hour He never leaves
With eyes you can feel but cannot see
Rest assured that He always looks upon you and me.

Never Really Lost

I lost someone but
Did they really lose me?

My nights are cold and
Without you just lonely

But I keep getting this thought
In the back of my mind

That you're absent from this life
But never erased from time

So, maybe there could be
A better place to be…

I lost someone
But did they really lose me?

John 11:25-26

Jesus said unto her, "I am the resurrection, and the life: he that believeth in me, though he were dead, yet shall live, and whosoever liveth and believeth in me shall never die"…

BARABBAS IS FREE

Benson Odenge (bensonodenge@gmail.com)

Yours is a case prima facie as you stand in the dock
Perhaps you murdered in mugging escapades
Maybe you silenced a government functionary
You were cheered on as a luminary

You by reason of oppression stand accused of treason
A gamut of witnesses you face
Who unravel your deeds to your face

Men you've maimed, women you've widowed
Traders you've plundered
Kids you've orphaned, all for your disgruntlement
Each with a sorry story to tell

Guilty as charged, the verdict goes
With no mitigating plea
Into the dungeon you go, that dark some abode
That cell that clobbers the mental you

And there in the gloom
A soldier you love to hate emerges
The burly beast beckons you
Before the judge he leads you
A petrified version of you
A barrage of puzzles flood your mind

Voila!

Subdued is the judge, by reason of the grudge
Of the rowdy crowd Barabbas is free
Since Jesus paid the price upon the tree

And took upon him Barabbas' curse
For cursed is he, I say, who hangs on a tree
Upon whom my guilt I lay
Who upon the wood he did me good

Barabbas is yours truly.

Mark 15:15

Wanting to satisfy the crowd, Pilate released Barabbas to them. He had Jesus flogged, and handed him over to be crucified...

Into The Night

Moving away from your comfort zone
You're stepping out into the night

I am the element of uncertainty
I chill the spine as you walk out into me

Who is nearby lurking? What's brewing in the air?
What secret force wants to pull you into their lair?

A terror that stalks by night
Or
Cerebral creatures ascending from the highest height

Whatever unfolds, cascades, or beholds
Their advantage is dark timing

For the envelope is now open
Time to give-up or fight

These are the apparent truths
About stepping out into the night.

Psalm 119:105

Thy word is a lamp unto my feet, and a light unto my path

1Hundred 44 Thousand

We were all just trying to make it

But what's in the heart cannot be hidden

Although the outer facade might try to fake it

A special 144,000 will be the ones that make it in.

Revelation 7-8

...And I heard how many were marked with the seal of God—
144,000 were sealed from all the tribes of Israel...

Wake Up Call

N. A. Selvy

It seems like we're living in perilous times
Spirits are being broken
And many are troubled of the mind

So.. how can one's dream
Keep from dying?
When it's looking like the mountain
Ain't even worth climbing

Young fatherless boys are searching
To fill empty voids
And they're constantly being told
It's in earthy possessions like fast money & cars

Blinded by
Materialism and fleshly desires
While pride, greed and anger
Got em' playing with deadly fires

Millions of souls are being set up
For eternal burning
And the babies are having babies
So who's teaching and who's learning?

It seems they're being programmed
By the lies portrayed on radio, social media & TV.

As the demonic forces that were chanting
"Surrender your soul" subliminally
are now coming straight at them bold & aggressively

The young girls are growing up
Wanting to look like celebrities & stars
So they go in bathrooms secretly
To throw up the food they just bought

While some are playing manipulative games of the mind
As they're chasing those dollar signs
Trying to see who will be the next funder
Of their enhanced body parts...

Doing anything they can
Just to rid themselves of flaws
(But I'm sorry honey) neither a designer purse
Cute fitted shirt or tight mini skirt
Can be a cover up for all of those mental scars

It's sad that even some parents won't
Focus more on their kids
Because they're out here trying to keep up
With their OWN false images

Can't you see that love, guidance and correction
Is what our children really need?
But instead.. these broken homes
Are forcing them into the streets

So they're struggling
To fix what they think
Are external problems
That actually started internally

What sad sight to see
Things are getting out of hand
It's going too far
So I'm doing the best I can to sound the alarm
Because there's definitely a need for
A WAKE UP CALL

I can't break it down y'all
No better than this
Lets come together and take a stand
Against the disorder that's in our midst

Where there is no vision
The people will surely perish
This is not a game
One wrong move
And there's no coming back from it

So I make a plea
To those of you who
Know within your heart
That you really need to

STOP living life carelessly

Before you get pulled deeper into the deep
Deceptively believing that you're soaring with eagles
When you ain't even flying with birds

Because you'll be too confused in the mind
To realize
That you've been weighed down
By all that junk your soul has incurred

Don't you know

That without knowledge of the truth
Your sight will forever be blurred???
Now that's a word
To the wise
And if this is speaking to you
I pray it opens your spiritual eyes

Because whether you believe it or not
There will one day be an end to this life
And I don't know about you
But it matters where my soul ends up
When it reaches the other side..

More than anything
I wanna see my Heavenly Father
When I leave here
And if you're somewhat concerned
You'd better get to know Him

For the riches of this life
Will one day be to no avail
So ask yourself this final question..
Will avoiding the narrow way and taking the wide path
Really be worth living out
An Eternal sentence in a FLAMED Cell???

Well...

I hope you make the right decision
So the ultimate test you won't fail
Because trust and believe
Texas heat in the summer
Ain't got NOTHING on that FIRE
THAT'S BREWING IN HELL!!!

I'm not trying to scare you,
Just sounding the alarm
Hoping and praying that whomever's listening..

WILL take heed to THIS WAKE UP CALL

Ephesians 5:14

...14 This is why it is said,
"Wake up sleeper, rise from the dead,
and Christ will shine on you"

SIGHT

On a truly dark day in a truly dark year
In the darkest pit of my life
I had actually reached the point
Where I mindfully lost my sight

The hardest thing was finding it again, while blind
The hardest thing was leaving the *true* light behind

It was only after I dealt with the darkness
That things began to turn right
With a particular state of mind
I was slowly able to find
The brightest way to leave the darkness behind.

Ephesians 5:8-13

For you were once darkness, but now you are light in the Lord. Live as children of light 9 (for the fruit of the light consists in all goodness, righteousness and truth) 10 and find out what pleases the Lord. 11 Have nothing to do with the fruitless deeds of darkness, but rather expose them. .. 13 But everything exposed by the light becomes visible...

Divided By 3 Squared

Uncomfortably comfortable, squared by the room we're in
Being here is my delight even though something is never quite right

The way you treat me has got to be a sin
You always screw me over and pin me in

You know just how to catch my weakness

Out of everyone I've met you hold the record as the meanest
You brute. You abuser. You lying accuser
You disrespectful, narcissistic user!

Mathematically 'squared' means that the exponent is 2

Regardless of what the base is between me and you
What can this be? Why does it always feel like there's three?
You, me- and some other evil entity

Three squared equals nine which is just about the time
You spin out of control and your virtues unwind
How we always ended up here is really just a blur
I remember when you appeared
It made me believe that miracles truly do occur

But, who needs a miracle if it leaves you feeling like this?
I thought I'd heard from God but maybe there's something I've missed
The content of your character could only come from Sheol
For the mouth explicitly speaks what the heart sees as real

You make sure that only you can win
That's how I've ended up trapped here all over again
Uncomfortably comfortable squared by the room we are in.

The Human Heart

Down a dormant alley of the hurting beating heart
A clot of angst has nestled in to block a vibrant new start
Since it is written that God has placed eternity in the hearts of man
Then intuitively we know that our dreams
Can expand like grains of sand
So, eternally a dream will out last a woman or man

Therein, we are eternal by nature, but that is not all
History still reminds us that there was a great human fall
At the beginning of time there was one named Eve the other Adam
Where would we be without this story about them?
Because of *them* are we so wretched and impure?
Because of *us*, each year proves it more and more

So what will it be, humanity?
Could we ever change or were we always destined for calamity?
Each one has a dead zone in the arches of their beating heart
This brings us all together, yet keeps us worlds apart

Funny how we are so much the same, but no one is alike
We struggle up each mountain hike
Not realizing that if we just rented a two-seated trike
We'd make it up the hill *together*

Together is key to making the world better
Tonight let's keep hope alive and beating in our hearts forever
And maybe we'll see a change… on the 25th of never.

Psalm 4:4

Be angry, yet do not sin;
on your bed, search your heart and be still.

A Start

Morning creeps in with every tick of the clock
Just like each one of our heart beats

At some hour will stop
Both mysteriously numbered
And we live somewhere in between
With each end is a new beginning
It's a circle constantly spinning
We exist somewhere in between
A mundane life with divine spiritual meaning

How do we know what will happen next?
On our own we're too comfortable
Seeking what *we* think is best
We all are like sheep
From the greatest to the least

We no not
What we know not
And the wisdom we think we have
We really don't got
We need guidance to find what is *true* truth
We need a lesson that's goes deeper
Than basic human roots.

Hard Hope

Hope is really hard
Hard to develop and hard to keep
Especially in the midnight hour
When you've had more worry than sleep

It almost makes you dread the coming new day
Since you haven't had a breakthrough, even if and when you pray
The miracle of an answer still neglects to look your way

I never plan to feel like this especially when I wake up
The teachers are preaching, the new choir is singing
But nothing has changed... I'm still stuck!

Does anyone know the remedy for times like this?
If not, then I'll just call it 'life'
Where some of us win and some just get dismissed.

Just Past
The Graveyard

There's silence across the graveyard, but quiet is just a notion

When you walk this path through the soft loose grass
It tinges on every sense of emotion
Does this place offer a serene reward for the inhabitants the Earth is
trapping? Or is this just a stage we call 'the grave' where everyone is
Merely napping?

Our eyes look over headstones and rolling mounds of grass
As our minds drift off in wonder as we silently ride past
Here, you've spent life's last token taking you to a land unspoken
For the cemetery can be a scary place since an unknown chapter has
Awoken
Honestly, how ever long the gate may be, I always try to scurry by
Hey! Maybe you do something too like hold your breath or close your
eyes! Whatever you've grown accustomed to
I'm not here to judge your disguise

Because we all see it as the eeriest of places
We imagine the uncanny looks of ghostly pale faces
But the true terror we hold is really just a reminder to us all

That one day you and I will also experience that six foot fall

The terror of *not* knowing when your own name will be called

But there's a different perspective if you can see beyond the surface

The true scary part is not the grave, it's finding out you wasted time

Not fulfilling your life's purpose.

Ecclesiastes 3:1-8
There is a time for everything, and a season for every activity under
the Heavens...

Luna

Above the earth's surface all alone at night
Like a button that fastens the sky's cloak tight
I watch from a distance just to see what will be
The brightness of me is all that you see
As each earthling eye looks up at me
With wonder and curiosity

I have another side that's exclusively unknown
Another side that's rarely shown
This side has turned its face away from the Earth
Hiding from the corruption until it's rebirthed

Hanging here at the gravity of obedience
The Lord set me in place with duty and allegiance
With each phase of my orbit, I'm aching and forlorn
If I had it my way I'd leave you shaken and torn

The years of brutality have taken their toll on me
You could never imagine just what I've seen
I remain a distant whiteness, a silent record keeper
Night after night Earth's display grows bleaker
Sometimes I stick around to watch when it's day

I converse with the sun to see if he feels the same way
Yet the Earth is blessed whenever I come out
I was told to brighten the shadows when the main light is out

I push sea waves, start seasons, and end days
I turn blood red then black out in cycles as if I'm dead
Incomprehensible signs, passing you by unread

The schedule is set for my light to fall dim
For the New Jerusalem will only need to be lit by HIM
So take a good look at me now while you can
Because the next time I rise upon this land

Could be the last time you ever see my face again.

I Am Why

I'm reaching out to show you a place, come with me now to find this space.

Yes, at times life seems so very tough, and stress levels show that you're dealing with more than enough. You've lost all that you had, you're a mile beyond mad, and grief has taken you far beyond being sad.

It's human nature to direct your anger at me. But do remember, there's more to life than just what the eyes can see. *I AM, the only cure.* The antidote to ease each and every sore. When you cast your burdens to me I have something to exchange. Peace in the storm will help to rearrange… The way you think or how you feel. I have the cure and prayer is part of that deal. What you're doing is called life, it's perfectly designed this way. You're a fragile human being but you're given help each day. Trust me my child, I am the one who settles all scores. When you invite me into the situation, remarkably it is no longer *just* yours.

Trust and believe, life is greater than just what you see, for you have only been told 1% about me. You can't even imagine every possibility. The joy of the Lord can be your strength, pain will not conquer you at any length. The life you experience is a temporary time. Everybody with a beginning will one day leave all that they know behind. Things you see now can all be destroyed, everything around you shows that there is life beyond this void. I will walk with you in uncertain waves and on the sunny sea shore of pleasant days. You were created to need God now and forever more, that is exactly why I'm telling you all of this for.

Although your life may seem like a mess, it's designed in steps, just like the process of getting dressed. There are seasons in all things, so I need you to see that all needs are found primarily in me. Even when the storms of life crash in so violently. Take root in me, I am that ancient tree. I am coming soon and my reward is with me, for I Am life abundantly.

I AM the Source

The First

The Last

In all eternity of course

Life and all that will ever be

Begins and ends precisely with me.

John 1:4

In Him was life, and that life was the light of men

After

Lying here half alive, half awake

And if the morning should come

Do not try to revive me

I'm still awake feeling the burn of heartache

The sunlight will only remind me

If it's true that you come looking for your missing sheep

Then I tell you 're wasting your time

For after all that my life has seen

Being a good sheep is the last thing on my mind

This world is full of choices we all will have to make

And this is a burden no one should have to take

So I just want to lay here

Half alive, half awake.

Romans 8:18

For I reckon that the sufferings of this present time are not worthy to be compared with the Glory which shall be revealed in us.

One Bright Star

A person's gift makes room for them and brings them before great people

Uncountable galaxies fan across outer space
Each one has a name and it's own designated place
Piercing through an endless open black sea
Came one bright shining star that everyone could see
Unfortunately, this star could not recognize its own brightness
It's beauty and worth he couldn't see in the slightest

Sighing out loud it exclaimed through a tear
Gosh, *there are so many good looking stars out here*!
How can I compare with other gems in this sea
When each one is so uniquely opposite of me?
Now listen to me, low self esteem can be expected
When we live outward verses looking within
You can feel like a loser watching everyone else win
But don't forget you are a *star* and you have a special place
You're a very important piece that makes up the entire human race

So the next time you're down and you've lost who you are
Just look up in the night and find the brightest shining star
Let it be a reminder that uniqueness is a gift, a talent that's God given
You were made this way to fulfill your purpose and His vision.

Shooting Stars

It's said that if you wish upon a star just right
Your dreams true and indeed they just might
Outside I saw a shooting star that night
And turned around ignoring its flight

I went in the house and closed the door, but my eyes
Caught the sudden glimpse of two more
Shrugging it off I brushed my teeth
And slowly dropped my nightgown on the floor

Then out of the gown popped the two stars
Twinkling and shining so bright
I had to blink twice just to make sure I was clearly seeing this right

So quickly they flashed bouncing up and down
Then fizzled out as if they were never around

I realized the night is such an unknown mystery
The life of creation stretches far beyond what the eye can see.

Psalms 65:8

The whole earth is filled with awe at your wonders;
where morning dawns, where evening fades, you call forth songs of joy.

The Man

Among The Myrtle Trees

Tick-skip, Tick-Tock this is the Earth's sound when no one is around
As the planet keeps spinning around and round
At the edge of the world on a breezy sunny day
I sat beneath a tree as the wind began to sway

As I watched the clouds tumble across the sky

A man of honor appeared and I stood up to say hi
He walked among the myrtle trees, down a path I hadn't noticed before
His steps were smooth, steady as the breeze
For he wasn't even touching the floor

He lifted his arms and pointed to the path, one on the left and right
Without speaking a word he told me things, full of glory and might
Enlightened, my eyes were opened, in my mind he had planted a seed

The path you choose is up to you, my direction you'd best take heed

He blew into me the *way* mixed with truth and life
He gave me vital lessons that are sure to help me avoid strife
As the trees began to sway in the pleasant breeze that started to blow
He tilted his hat with a gentle smile to signal it was his time to go

I watched him walk among the myrtle trees then vanish into thin air
But the peace he left behind assured me that he was really there.

Zechariah 1:8-11

I saw at night, and behold, a man was riding on a red horse, and he
was standing among the myrtle trees which were in the ravine, with
red, sorrel, and white horses behind him...

Avenue See

If you decide to ride past you're neglecting yourself a treat
For when you turn right and drive all the way to the end of this street
You'll discover your perspective of humanity
Will either be undone or complete

The sights you'll find that naturally combine
This spot, where chills enliven the curve of your spine
Earth meets art in a voiceless poetic speech
Revealing the creator's expertise for expressive techniques
The only spot where a piece of Heaven touches the Earth
The kind of place that lets you know this world has a special worth

What a sight to see be it night or day
Unfolding dimensions and mountains joined together this way
There is a beauty when Heaven and Earth combine
This kind of wonder could only be forged by the hand of Father time.

Jeremiah 32:17
Ah, Sovereign Lord, you have made the heavens and the earth by
your great power and outstretched arm. Nothing is too hard for you.

116

The Earth Thou Art

In the still of the night when the moon was full and bright
I listened to the harmony of nature all around me
As the trees swayed in the gentle breeze
They reminded me that life can have a rhythm of ease

I observed the trees growing upwards, poised in frozen physique
As the mysterious words of the Bible they suddenly began to speak
He sends the rains and snow to fulfill their purpose and it causes the
Earth to sprout. The rain and snow do not return to Him without
fulfilling the purposes He chose to bring about

Under my feet the rocks sat in their position as the moonlight
Gracefully hit them I could tell they were on a mission
They begin echoing in monotone and sing out a glorious hymn

"If the people keep silent, we rocks will
cry out again to worship Him"

This was their chant as they laid there flat on the surface
From the sky to the ground nothing could keep their praises bound
As their faces stared up to the heavens day and night rain or shine
Witnessing this display burned sweetly into my mind

Nature shows us how God's creation shares their love
And it taught me how to keep my eyes *set* on the things that are
Above.

1 Chronicles 16:33

Then shall the trees of the forest sing for joy before the Lord,
for he comes to judge the earth.

117

Awakening Genesis
Madyanis Santiago Díaz

The curiosity of the beginning dwells in the emptiness
Where nothing existed before clusters of stars arrived

Yet, it is so intriguing to realize existence's endlessness
While the effervescent flow of creativity seems to strive

Pushing our firsts steps guided by nature's impulse
Hence the birthing five elements feed our new paths

That is where our innocent hearts follow their pulse
Awakening to the melodic birth of a magnificent wrath.

(madyanissantiago@yahoo.com)

A Bliss That Ever Lasts

Madyanis Santiago Díaz

To see your authentic eyes penetrate my enchanted soul
Is to live my dream incarnated into an angelic mold

To feel your luring touch as I protect your loving heart
Is to feel the heavens enclose me into a bliss that ever lasts

When you stay next to me while we hear the birds sing
My soul finds perfection in the musical notes of your heartbeat

And as abundant fruits await on our starry dining table
My mouth only wants to enjoy the essence of your flavor

Tell me to recite my poetry while you lie down in my arms
And I will engage in writing verses on your skinned lands

Tell me to envision the eternity of unconditional love by your side
And I will make the wind write on the sky that you are mine.

The Wilderness Stream

Above a rushing brook in the cool of the ice
In the baby blue glow of the freshly fallen snow
The moon reflects its light in the water's enchanting flow
Twas there I saw a deer, he appeared to me as gentle as a Lamb

A powerful burst of majestic spirit floats softly on the midnight air
alone in the wilderness with no fear
For the Living God is drawing near
The power of his might, the invincibility of this night
I feel the royal courts gathering all around
And though my eyes may search
In *spirit* is the only place this wonder can be found
Heavenly hosts and majestic breezes, Cherubim hover and sing
The essence of God appears in this
Extraordinary display of holy things

My human mind can't figure it out but my soul leaps with joy
For it knows what this is all about
Engulfed in a heavenly dream, to what do I credit this pleasure?
How lucky of me to be blessed with such a wonderland treasure
Last thing I remember is climbing into bed ranting and raving with a
heart full of dread, for something in me was spiritually dead
But now that I'm asleep, I am *finally* awake

Out here alone in the snowy trees naked and vulnerable
But yet I do not freeze

Full of shame, my thoughts made God the blame, but transformation
I see since he came to blow breath on me, I'm *finally* set free
From the stagnation of mental misery
Twas naked I was, free of guilt or shame, although dreaming I knew
I was forever changed.
He clothed me in love and grace was the guide
He took with him my ego and smashed my pride

Above a rushing brook, in the cool of the moonlight
I'm standing in the baby blue glow of the freshly fallen snow
The moon reflecting in the water's enchanting flow
Twas there I saw the deer, He appeared to me as gentle as a Lamb.

Boy In The Stars

I stared up at the stars one night and glimpsed a peculiar set of eight
Strange sights can be seen when you're up really early or even late
For chiseled in the dark expanse, I had to blink twice to see
Within this set of stars was a galaxy boy waving back at me

He spoke to me in twinkles, a celestial Morris Code
I tried to look away but his presence was awfully bold
The wonder high above me was quite a sight to see
His existence felt like purpose as he looked in the window at me

I started to question my sanity as I was already feeling quite sleepy
I looked again and there he was, friendly but still slightly creepy
He solemnly danced on the milky way and enjoyed the night before
the break of day, so I watched him twinkle until the dawn
Then he slowly started to look withdrawn

Yet, all that mattered on that night was his and my connection
Waving goodbye he took a bow
Leaving a disappearing act of perfection

The night he saw me and I saw him, in one thing
I will always be certain the galaxy boy appears to cheer
Those night hearts who have been hurting.

Psalm 119:148

My eyes anticipate the night watches, that I may meditate on your word

HEAVEN

Syreeta Adams, WSYI

Imagine days full of turmoil to the joy of soul purpose

Heaven

Think past the troubles of yesterday and find joy in a new day

Heaven

Figure tomorrow full of right choices and rest in the lessons learned today

Heaven

Explore life here on earth, in peace, love, joy, and happiness

Heaven

(whateverskinyourin@simplyugmo.com)

Just "B" And Believe

Syreeta Adams, WSYI

The craftiness of an enemy is avoidable by distance
But what to do when you're unaware of resistance?

Trust in the fact that your purpose knows the strategy

Just submit to the will of creation
Resist the urge to entertain the inner-me

B-Present. **B**-Free. **B**-Joyfull. **B**-Happy. **B**-Faithful

And **B**elieve!

(whateverskinyourin@simplyugmo.com)

Waiting For You

I'll be waiting for you where tiny buds of sunshine grow
The place where yellow butterflies set green fields aglow
The place the heart knows but only in time will the eyes get to see
The place my soul calls *home*... somewhere in eternity

I *promise* to be waiting for you where buds of sunshine grow
The place where happiness and harmony abound
In an uninterrupted flow
Promise you will *look for me* over by the sycamore tree
On a beach of mystic sand with a giant sun hat
And a frosty Pineapple drink in my hand
I'll be right there relaxing in a straw lawn chair
Grateful for the moment when I'm finally free from worries and cares

You'll know you're in the right place because the ocean will be a
breathtaking blue, fading into hints of turquoise and white
To welcome a weary soul like you
The waves will dance so gloriously
And I'll marvel at the sight my eyes will finally see

I'll stay right there watching the moonlight
Until the dawn chases away the star filled night

Only to reveal the second glorious day
As the sun stretches itself across the bay
At that hour I'll finally emerge from my hat to say
"The weather is perfect in *Heaven* today!"

Imagine with me, where you might find yourself to be
On the first morning *after* this life sets you free.

1 Corinthians 2:9
Eye has not seen, nor ear heard, nor have it entered into the heart of
man, the things which God has prepared for those who love Him.

Surf The Galaxy

Come away with me for just one night
I've already got your ticket
And you'll only be gone until daylight
So hurry up let's not miss this
Come take my hand we'll go up, up

Up to a distant land
We'll catch a ride, on the fastest shooting star we'll soar
That takes us into the Heavens
To knock on God's Kingdom door

On the way back down we'll catch a bite to eat
We can scoop up some Milky Way
And sit on crest of the moon to dangle our feet
As we happily enjoy our galaxy treat

As the time draws near
We'll hop on the clouds that are white not clear
As we inhale the smell of a rising that's new
We'll drink from the clouds that drop the fresh morning dew

Before we go, we'll sit at the top of a perfect rainbow

To get the right angle at just the right hour
To catch the sun peek through with amazing fire power
Then as the night mist starts to wade
And the stars go away and the shadows fade
We'll float back home in the dawn's parade
Then wake up to realize

What a pleasant dream we've made.

Proverbs 27:17

As iron sharpens iron, so a friend sharpens a friend.

Dark Before Dawn

On the first day of winter I arose early with my tea
When on the bare maple branch sat a fluffy snow owl looking down at
me; I got entangled in his yellow hunter eyes
His puffy white feathers outlined his size

I was highly aware Twas the dark before dawn
A time when impossible feats seem to go on
For it is said that this hour holds one minute of magic
Since it was that time our meeting was dramatic

Locked in together his face with mine
We were bound in that moment for this special period of time
And just before our one minute would stop
A spec of light warned us the sun was coming up
But in the last couple seconds he belted out one word
The wisdom of nature from this mystic snow bird
Adonai!
He shrieked and away he flew
This word Means 'My Lord' in Hebrew
The creator made us all, and even *he* knew
Everything that we say matters, so speak what is true.

Romans 15:13

May the God of hope fill you each day with all the joy and peace as you
trust in him so that you may overflow with hope by
the power of the Holy Spirit

Moon Dance

Sleeping under the blanket of midnight silver and blue
Coated in lunar illumination that is only produced by you

Parked high above the planet I peek through my window at your
Display and I wonder to myself, should I step out of my covered place
And into your brilliant array?

This night is calling me as the dark coincides with your flow
I'm pulled out in the open, and into your enchanted glow
Do you see me standing here as I gaze up at you?
With pride you dominate the night sky as God instructed you to
Whenever you appear your presence makes my heart sing
Your lunar effect makes the night perfect
As I admire the glow of your outermost ring

Has the Earth captured you just like your appearance detains me?
The balancing act between us helps sustain all of the life you see
So I will tell you this as we stare face to face
You've brightened our world and you can not be replaced

So, I'll sing out an orchestra, my lullaby composed of you in song
Two dancing elements shall always remember their bond
Since me to you, and you to me is obviously so very fond
One thing I must declare as I stand refreshed in your perfect light

The sun shall not smite me by day, nor *you* moon by night.

Romans 1:20

For his invisible attributes, namely, his eternal power and divine nature, have been clearly perceived, ever since the creation of the world, in the things that have been made.

So they are without excuse.

Bible Nights

☆In the midst of the dark *Paul* and *Silas* agree that praise will be their midnight melody. Then out of the sky a powerful light shines and frees them from their prison confines

☆In a moonlit field *Jacob* is in a tussle, he wrestles an *Angel* of might and muscle. Nearing the end his side is struck, yet he was still blessed before the sun came up

☆Hour of terror for the Hebrew first born, a Passover spirit comes to kill with scorn. But if you're covered under the blood of the lamb, this night you'll be protected by the *Great I Am*

☆By day it was cloud by night pillar of fire. Heavenly direction in hopes to inspire *Israelite* faith that Jehovah God is with us; 40 years of wandering resulted from distrust

☆Cool night air blows on a newborn's face, surrounded by people and animals from all over the place. Behold, the brightest star is shining on top of the earth. This marks the blessed night of *Jesus'* birth

☆Desperately trying to hold back the sorrow, seeking prayer hoping to escape tomorrow. Into the garden the disciples go; *Gethsemane* is the place where Jesus let his emotions flow

☆Samuel! *Samuel*! Called the voice in the night. He rose to his feet and to service took flight. But to his surprise it was a bigger call, *God* came in the night to explain a future downfall

☆Seizing the moment at just the right time, stepping out before dawn, a quiet place He must find. *Jesus* took the morning and went out to pray, seeking the *Father* before the first light of day

☆Hurricane winds began to blow, violently churning the water just right. For the disciples were caught in the middle of a storm, stirring the boat after midnight. Surprise! Across the water the son of God is here, turning eyes from panic and calming the sea of fear

☆A covenant made in the dim moon light while *Abraham* rests on a hillside at night. *Your future descendants will outnumber the stars.*
A promise kept during his time and ours.

Psalm 104:34
My meditation of him shall be sweet

O, Prisoner In Chains

Oh I'm bound in the most existential way
By a deeper love that dwells night and day
Trapped in chains but I would have it no other way

To you, what happened to me looks wrong
But to me, it's oh so very right
For I am a prisoner in chains
Who advocates for eternal life

Bound by a deeper love
For the one and only Jesus Christ.

Ephesians 4: 1

As a prisoner for the Lord, then, I urge you to live a life worthy of
the calling you have received.

He Carried Me

As night falls again I bow my head
And clasp my hands
To give the Father thanks for his grace and mercy

Still feeling all of the pain
Still constantly wondering why
Yet, still recognizing my blessings
And lifting His name on high

I still cry
But He wipes my tears
I'm still afraid
But He calms my fears
I still wonder if He really hears

But when I hit rock bottom
I remember the footprints in the sand
I know that He carries me
At times when I can't even stand.

Isaiah 26:3
You will keep him in perfect peace, whose mind is stayed on You
because he trusts in You.

DESTROY

Wall sitting creatures that lurk in dark shadow places
I bind you in chains and blind the eyes on your faces
To every witch and warlock too
There's no spirit you can conjure
Where the name of Jesus won't destroy you

Every one legged creature that deploys from the woods
Any wicked ghost or demonic spirit who's up to no good
I arrest your authority and dish out a spiritual whipping
I lose you now from the evil you're committing

I take out my double edge sword
To dice you up using the name of the Lord
I burn you with *holy fire* and cast you to the pit
Your plans are now spoiled
You won't move forward with any of it

For I bathe in the precious blood of The Lamb
I bow at the altar of the Great I AM
I crack the whip and break every chain
I send forth Waring Angels to highly proclaim
There's great strength and power when you call on the highest name

King Jesus' Authority Will Forever Remain.

Ephesians 6:11-13

For our struggle is not against flesh and blood, but against the rulers, against the authorities, against the powers of this world's darkness, and against the spiritual forces of evil in the heavenly realms.

Divine Construction

It started with a tiny speck of silver on my black construction paper
I envisioned a fine sight with tiny specks of illumination, starlight
I said it was good, this is starting off right
Then I went ahead and separated the day from night

I continued to work on the very next day
Creating a divide, I folded the paper, half on each side
Now two worlds were formed from the construction of one
I set my mind to see what else could be done
At the bottom half, I spoke the sea in one command
Then I rolled back the liquid to reveal dry land

Full of creativity I filled the waters with creatures of plenty
Upon the land I made the animals, unique and many
Now that a variety of creatures roam the liquid, land, and sky
I marveled at the beauty emerging from the twinkle in my eye
I set the day spring in place, closed the door between time and space
Then I planned to make the next day so wonderfully full of grace

There was only one thing missing, a creation I could claim as mine
So, on the sixth day I reached down and touch the Earth's clay

To mold a man quaint in the image of Yahweh

In a sacred spot that only I knew, I breathed life into his lungs and the Vessel came to! Now, what on Earth do I finally see?

A piece of Heaven made in the image of me.

Genesis 1:26-27

Then God said, "Let Us make man in our image, after our likeness..."

Watch Hour Prayer

Could you meet me after midnight
The time is twelve O'one
When the crickets silence their chirping
And the first half of night is done

Meet me after midnight as
The hairs on my back take chill
Children of God contend in prayer
Challenging the dark kingdom's surging will

Realms of wonder fight forces of light
Picking on the vulnerable corrupting their sight
Let the sleeping sleepers lie
As unknown threats fly through an ash filled sky
Hope comes on the wings of fresh morning air
Reminding us all that our salvation has never left us bare

But just for a moment at 4:02
Victory broke and old things become new
For that special reason I asked could we meet
To hold hands in victory and rejoice in defeat
Since the morning has awoken, I've seen evil retreat
We now have two hours left, so let's go back to sleep!

Psalm 119:62
At midnight I shall rise to give thanks to You...

Co-in-ci-dence

So you think it's a coincidence that you're awake now

It's a spiritual hour, yet you still can't see how

Destiny and fate are both as close as a prayer

But you won't even speak a whisper

Or part your lips to go there

Do you think the bewitching hour

Is for everyone else *but* you?

Or maybe you're still convincing yourself

This phrase just isn't true

Did you ever stop to wonder if this is the exact hour

The second coming is upon you

And Jesus returns with an Angel army of power?

You might wanna be wise and take this a gamble

Since your already in too deep

The next time you wake at three AM

A prayer of direction is what you should seek.

Matthew 25:6

And at midnight there was a cry made, behold, the bridegroom cometh;
go out to meet him.

Silence Speaks

In the still of silence God *is* actually speaking
In the still of solace I wait to see if this holds true
The darkness behind my eyes reflects my inner blue
Where emotionally I linger hoping to catch a moment with you

Your honorable name is muttered while my lonely lips are trembling
In the still I lie in wait to see if your angels are assembling
Just a whisper, a hum, any word will do
To sustain my faith while waiting upon you
But all I hear is silence as my heart skips a beat
I fidget around and anxiously move my feet

Heavy and daunting is this persistent SILENCE
That moves me to question my faith in lonesome defiance
My mental noncompliance becomes perfectly clear
As this steady hush is casting light on my fear

Oh God, come near!
I'm waiting on my knees wondering if I did something wrong
I long for your voice so no wait is too long
I cry out again thinking now's the right time
But you say not a word, your mystery is so divine

In the hours I've spent focusing on the *absence* of your voice
I've finally come to realize it was actually a negative choice
This whole time I have been pulling out my hair
I didn't see that God was already there
Speaking through silence so loud and clear
Sending comforting vibes to my listening ear

I just couldn't hear it, since I was waiting for an audible voice
I completely forgot that communication comes
With more than just one choice

Regretting the human stipulations that
I placed on Him from the start
I learned to listen without using my ears
To the silence that accompanies a beating heart.

God is always speaking so leave yourself an open door.
You may not realize what the silence is for, but it's in these
moments where He is speaking all the more.

Star Shifter

In the assignment of a Star Shifter

Nothing can be as it remains
Prayer moves mountains, mysteries
Emerge from deeply hidden fountains
And all circumstances can be rearranged

Oh Book of Ancient words so easily skipped by
Guide my hand through the stars
As I rotate and turn destiny over in the sky
Power given because I am me made by HE
I bind and loose to fulfill a desired destiny

Star Shifter, Fate Twister, Boundless Burden Lifter
At the hour a midnight evil encroaches from the dark
I am the beacon, shining His light from my heart.

Psalm 134:1
Bless the Lord, all servants who serve by night in the house of the Lord!

Breathe

I pray that the softness of Angel's feathers would come upon my heart Let me feel the love of an almighty hero who skillfully crafted this idea of life from the start. Please soften and change me by melting away the negativity I don't need-

Breathe, in and out, *Shalom*

With this prayer I know that I am being heard. With this prayer wrap me in the peace of your unspoken word. Like a heavenly field of the softest cotton, covering me like a warm hug on a cold night. Touch my mind and let me experience joy from a supernatural origin, as I arise and receive your glory while it's being poured in-

Breathe, in and out, *Shalom*

Blow upon me a gentle mist of angelic fragrance, the sweet elegance of internal happiness. Gently rock my senses back to everlasting life. Pour into my home the radiance of protection and fill the atmosphere with an essence of affection-

Breathe, in and out, *Shalom*

In every dimension our time is special, please inhabit this prayer as I softly speak. Peace be *still* in my heart. Peace be *still* in my thoughts. Peace be *still* all inner feelings that do not line up with this moment. May your anointing fall upon me like fresh golden honey, for the Comforter is near, I invite you to remain here-

Breathe, in and out

Amen.

Our Time Out

I'm allowed to take a sweet time out
A quiet pause to think about me
I never place a beginning or an end
On how long this vacation is supposed to be

For *here* is where I'm open to rest
And block out the entire world
For *here* is where we have our dance
Around and away we twirl

Asking questions, spending time
I silence the world because
I am His and He is mine

The presence of fellowship
Is what we have between us
Just Me, myself, and
The sweet presence of Jesus
Everything else is virtually meaningless.

1 Corinthians 6:17

But he who is joined to the Lord becomes one spirit with Him.

I Come Alive At Night

Like the exuberant feeling of warm daylight
My soul stands to attention and my heart lifts to take flight

For I am a *watchman* who comes alive at night

Since the Lord above never slumbers nor sleeps
The same goes for Satin and all of his nighttime creeps

I come alive to kill the midnight crow before the morn
I come alive to sound the Holy Shofar Horn

For how can I sleep when my enemy is awake?
Plotting through the night to plan the day's heartache

No!

I am a soldier and I come awake at night
Yielding non carnal weapons
Taking ground in the Lord's fight
For I am The *Watchman* who stands guard in prayer
And I come alive at the spike of midnight air.

Weep~In

The monster named heavy tries desperately to drown out our faith
But a soldier arises from within me that holds it in place

As I put to the side the events of the day
The pain of a loss, the struggle to pray
And everything else that went wrong today
With what I have left I will lift up to you
All the broken pieces my life has shattered into
I'm praying this is something you're willing to fix
Because I'm weak and tired and can't handle more of this

Right now all that's left is the strength to weep, so I'll weep to you
For there is no one else on earth worth weeping to

No one can take this burden but you
I heard it was said you comfort the weary
So, I'm trying this out (although I am leery)
I could use a refresh button or some brand new fresh air
I'm crying out to you in hopes that you really do care

I once heard that if we give our troubles to you
You'll transform a life and make someone new

So, if that's the case then tonight hear my plea
For there's a lot of people praying, I'm sure it's not just me

But, if you can hear through all other prayers
With all I have left I'm casting UP my cares

I will keep my eyes shut as I feel this hot tear fall
Just in case you're nearby and making house calls

The hope I have left I now place on you
I'll set my sights on tomorrow and pray to see something new.

Romans 15:13

May the God of hope fill you with all joy and peace as you trust in him…

153

Who Is He?

N. A. Selvy

Everyday the Heavens declare His Glory
By testifying of His Greatness
It shows the complexity of His knowledge
Which is Profoundly Amazing
And the works of His hands which are truly breathtaking

For, He is the Innovator of life
His hands sculptured dust
His breath gave life to Man

He's the Originator of all things
Designer of the blueprint
For the Universe's Master plan

Many say
He's the Unchangeable Changer
A Miraculous Marvel
For no book can contain the magnitude of His Wisdom
Because He is the Ultimate Author!

An Astonishing Wonder
Beyond anything we could ever comprehend
But yet, He's so intimate with us
That He knows every human being
And heavenly host personally by name and not one is missing!

It is He
Who gathered the waters
By holding them within the hollows of His hands

And with those same Illustrious prints
He marked off the Heavens with a span!

Yes, He all by Himself

Picked up the Mountains
And weighed them in scales
Look at the earth tremble in fear of Him
What a Mighty God we serve!

He's infinite in Power
For there's no limit to His abilities
Hear Him assuredly speaking in confidence Saying
"Lift up your eyes on high
And see who created these things!"

For it is He, that painted the sky
Put a fluff in the clouds
And placed boundaries around the sea
So we could stand upon a beaches' shore
To behold the splendor of His beauty

Are you still wondering...
Wondering who could HE be???

Well let me tell you
He's not only Wonderful,
Faithful and True

But He is Alpha and Omega
The Beginning and End
Accrediting those who trust in Him
By calling them His friend

He's a keeper of His Word
For He's not a man that He should lie
He's Gentle, Patient, Loving, Forgiving,
Merciful and Kind

He's Omniscient!
For the capacity of His Mastery is unknown
And He's Omnipresent
Because there's not a place too far
That He cannot reach or go

He's Omnipotent!
If He willed,
He could bring anything to past
That He choose
And He's The Most Sovereign God
For He is the One that truly rules!

Better yet! He is Agape Love
Sending His only begotten Son to die
So that the lost could be found
Come into repentance
And gain access to Everlasting Life

Yet, even if I had 10,000 tongues
I still wouldn't be able to express it all
So I'll conclude by saying
He's Divine in nature and Righteous
He's the Holiest One above them all

For He is The Incredible, Yet Indescribable One
Who's Mercy never fails or grows old
And He's patiently waiting with open arms
To welcome you in and be

A Multi Author Conglomeration

The Eternal Lover of your soul

Inspired by

Psalm 19 & Isaiah 40

Sleeping Peacefully

☆ A Passing Song ☆

Hear my prayer you've seen
What's happened there
As I cry out to you
I'm asking you to
Help me view things
Like you do

I'll wait on you Lord
To deal with the hurt
As sorrow drags me down
I'll wait on you Lord
To come touch my heart
And pick me off the ground

Peace of mind
Give me the strength to find
The beauty eyes can't see
All that you promised me
Heaven is my destiny
Peace of mind

Please help me Lord to find
A secret place in you
That you're calling me to
I need a special touch from you

Please help me Lord
To hear your voice
As Angels crowd around
Let your presence fall Surrounding us all
As glory's shining down

So I thank you Lord for Healing me
It's only you that sets us free.

John 11:25

Jesus told her,

" I am the resurrection and the life.

Anyone who believes in me will live,

even after dying."

Midnight Intercession

Never step into the night unless
You're fully covered under the blood
With night warfare hidden beings
Are roaming from below and above

Gilliack, Stacy, Necolah, and Jim
I don't know who you are but my spirit
Makes intercession for you from within

Out in the night random names shall I call
Praying that Satan will never destroy you all
Night intercession breaks bondages of sin
CoJack, Arnold, Havannah, and Tim
Under moonlight I plea for your Salvation

Ella, Zeet, Fitzgerald, Tomaca, and Pete
May night angels come and rescue you from defeat
Patel, Arnold, Benjamin, Anoka, and Lee
Around the world prayers setting midnight captives free.

160

Daniel 12:3

Those who are wise will shine like the brightness of the heavens, and those who lead many to righteousness, like the stars

forever and ever

For There Is Prayer

Prayer should have no end
Share your joys, your laughter, and your trials too
God created the world in a circle just to keep an eye on you

Prayer doesn't have to end at Amen
Take it on the go and speak like you're conversing with a friend
God won't reject you, and He hears anyone who chooses to call
He's with you even now to walk you through it all

Everything I've planned for you is already done
So let your spirit pay attention my precious one
I made a promise never to leave nor forsake
So cast me your burden, for then I will take-
Take your sorrow and exchange it for rejoicing
Turn your life around so you can feel my anointing

I am the I AM who restores all things
So have faith in me and see what it brings
Never stop praying for prayer changes things
It's your life line, your outreach, the way your soul sings

So pray it out while driving in your car
Talk to me about it no matter where you are
Prayer can take one thing and make it new
Prayer ushers in miracles specifically for you

I want to talk to you about your day
Lead your steps and show you the way
Prayer has been and currently will be
The supernatural channel to communicate with me.

Created 2Worship

Flames that consume but never burn
For it's you oh Lord for which I yearn

I long to know the truth, the truth of who you are
I burn to know your mysteries, mysteries beyond
Earth to the farthest star
My mind, my heart, and my soul beat steady yet out of control
Reaching, seeking, and dancing to a rhythm I long to know
I fear this feeling will all too soon pass since the one who aims
To put out my flames is prowling about and always on task

Draw near to my spirit as I call upon you, Lord
Show me how my prayers can fight back like a sword
Strengthen me to hold onto that spiritual flame
That stirs in my heart when I ponder your name

In life we have our ups and downs, our on and offs, and turnarounds
But if you ignite my *flame* it'll hold my ground
My desire is more than a fire for you
It's when deep calls unto deep that gets me more inspired by you
So I'll make it my vow to keep this light burning
Though the rain may fall and the wind is still churning
You are God above it all
That's why worshiping you *is* my God-given call.

Life's Battle Clothes

The Dawn Warrior's Anthem
Ephesians 6:13

At the start of this day and each day to come, I am involved in battle. It should be obvious that we do not wrestle against flesh and blood, because the battle never ceases.

Life is real, so before the sun rises, I must put on the Full Armor of God:

☆I put on and securely lace the **Shoes of the Gospel of Peace**, so that I can confidently walk around and conquer the enemies' grounds.

☆I strap on the **Belt of Truth** to help me stand firm in the truth of the word of God.

☆I place the **Breastplate of Righteousness** on my chest to keep my heart protected and pure from corruption and pain.

☆I pick up and fasten the **Shield of Faith** to hide me and absorb all the fiery darts and lies of Satan and his fellow workers of darkness.

☆I proudly place upon my head the **Helmet of Salvation** to seal in my confidence and stability, and protect my thoughts from fear, pollution, temptation, anxiety, or unbelief, etc.

☆I hold tight the **Sword of the Spirit** to cut down strongholds and expose the enemy to show the power and truth of the Lord.

Now Pray,

Heavenly Father,

I know that as children of God we are not fighting alone. I am a warrior ready and equipped for your army. I am dressed for battle by *your* authority. I have been given keys in the word of God for deliverance and I make the choice to exercise that power. I claim victory and with your help, I take over this day!

It's in Jesus name I pray,

Amen

Lamentations 2:19

Arise, cry aloud in the night. At the beginning of the night watches, Pour out your heart like water before the presence of the Lord, lift up your hands to Him...

The Good Book

Ever flowing, stuck
The water you can not drink
Ancient and vast mysteries
So prevalent it makes you think

Disastrous and brutal
Fierce, yet so secure
Treasures that last forever
Promising more and more

Stories, legends
History, tall-tails
Descriptive and precise
Making you look twice
Primitive times
Same human minds
One resource for many different kinds of binds

Sound off in my mind
The never ending song
Faith comes with deeper hearing
Even if you interpret it wrong.

Joshua 1:8

This book of the law shall not depart from your mouth, but you shall meditate on it day and night, so that you may be careful to do according to all that is written in it; for then you will make your way prosperous, and then you will have success.

Grace

You describe me as a fruitful vine
That the Father so lovingly tends to

I am pruned in season
Taken care of without reason
And my stem is a direct extension of you

For you are my root, my base
The reason I run this race
Without you I am nothing
Apart from you I can not do
The things my soul aspires to

You are firmly seated in the highest palace
Yet, your attention still expounds all around us
May your abundant ways stay for all of my days
And make my soul ever prosperous.

Colossians 2:7

Let your roots grow down into him, and let your lives be built on him. Then your faith will grow strong in the truth you were taught, and you will overflow with thankfulness

In Author Words

I must admit this book has truly been the most intimate experience I've had in writing. Many of these verses were created in the middle of the night, penned by the light of the moon. There were moments of angelic direction and special insights whispered by the subtle voice of God. When this project was first given to me, it reminded me of a modern-day book of Psalms. To expound upon the history of the book of Psalms, we must highlight the fact that it is an ancient Jewish songbook. It showcases prayers, complaints, praise, and petitions that make reverence to God. Over the centuries, God led various individuals to compose what comes across as *emotionally charged poems* which reflect on the heart of the human struggle.

I had to laugh because I realized that just like today, in ancient times they could proclaim *the struggle is real*, because it truly was! Also like today, many of us experience challenges and anguish in various different forms, and sometimes we need to find a way to vocalize it all. Many of us cry out for justice and make heartfelt pleas and laments to God in the night. Some of us are crying out for answers and grow tired of coming up short again and again. But like many of the Psalms, we must turn our hearts back to the theme of giving praise to our creator because everything truly begins and ends with God. He is most worthy, even if we feel contrary to that truth.

The things I've been through helped me learn how to turn to the Lord in all matters. From grandiose heartaches to happiness as small as the tiniest pebble. I've lived to see that He truly cares about it all. Lost in dark spaces he *always* found me. In times when my heart beat out of my chest with pounding terror, He *always* calmed me down. On weary nights when I had to find sleep under the stars, I could feel Him wrap a blanket around me and protect me from unknown surroundings (mentally and physically). So, this is why I can confidently affirm that He is there for you too. If you are struggling tonight, just know He hears you. There are so many mysteries and unimaginable aspects of our Jesus who intertwines with our existence, so you never know how close you are to a miracle.

Don't give up on your walk with him tonight- *don't* give up. You will be overjoyed that you pulled through in the end. Stay close to God. Hang on with all you've got, for just at the right time, he will reach in and lift you up so you can see that in Him all things truly are possible! I will be praying for you always.

Be blessed. Get rest. Know that God is *always* at His best.

In HIS Service,

*S*hamaira

The Voices of
A Distinguished Poet

Special thanks goes out to all of the talented poets and writers listed here!

Please realize that your contribution is part of a divine moment where Heaven's plans collided with Earth's inhabitants to create an everlasting masterpiece.

May all of the divine blessings that are attached to this book be attached to your lives forever & ever!

☆ **Benson Odenge**☆
(bensonodenge@gmail.com)

☆**Syreeta Adams**, WSYI☆
(whateverskinyourin@simplyugmo.com)

☆**Madyanis Santiago Díaz**☆
(madyanissantiago@yahoo.com)

☆**Jennifer Adams**☆
(angel23gp@hotmail.com)

☆ **N. A. Selvy** ☆

☆**Tamara G. Smith**☆

Midnight Meditations

For more information on Christian Inspirational Resources:

www.MidlifeRebirthProject.com

Midnight Meditations

A Multi Author Conglomeration

For A Unique Line of Kingdom Empowerment Apparel Visit:

www. Full-Armor-Gear .com

Midnight Meditations

Revelation 21:6

It is done.

I am the Alpha and the Omega

The Beginning and the End.

To the thirsty

I will give water without cost

From the spring of the water of life.

-Jesus Christ

Midnight Meditations